Psychology Spiritual

Adrian Collins

Copyright Page

First edition
All Rights Reserved
Author: © 2024, Adrian Collins

Index

The Path to Spiritual Awakening

The path to spiritual awakening is a deeply personal process that each individual navigates uniquely. Although it can sometimes seem like an abstract or mystical concept, in reality, spiritual awakening is simply the process of reconnecting with our deepest essence, that part of ourselves that transcends the daily noise of the mind and worldly concerns. It is a journey toward self-knowledge and full awareness of our existence. We often begin this journey when we feel like something is missing in our lives, as if what we have been chasing – success, money, recognition – is not fulfilling us in a lasting way. That feeling of emptiness or restlessness is often the spark that ignites spiritual awakening.

Spiritual awakening does not mean withdrawing from the world or becoming alienated from daily life. On the contrary, it is about engaging more fully in life, but from a more conscious place. It is learning to see life not only through the eyes of our needs and desires, but from a broader perspective, where we begin to perceive the world with more compassion, gratitude, and understanding. Spiritual awakening invites us to question our beliefs and thought patterns, those that we have learned since we were children and that, many times, limit us. It challenges us to see beyond the superficial and seek deeper answers about who we are and what our purpose in the world is.

Along this path, it is common to experience moments of confusion or uncertainty. Sometimes, we encounter obstacles or situations that seem to shake our way of seeing life. These challenges are, in fact, an essential part of spiritual awakening. They are opportunities to grow and learn, to leave behind outdated beliefs and open ourselves to new ways of being and thinking. This process does not happen overnight. In fact, it is something that can take years, even a lifetime. But the important thing is to understand that every small step counts. Every moment in which we decide to pay attention to our thoughts, emotions and actions, we are getting closer to awakening.

A fundamental part of the path to spiritual awakening is learning to live in the present. Our minds often tend to wander between the past and the future, which takes us away from the present moment, which is where life really happens. The practice of mindfulness helps us return to the here and now, where we can experience life more fully and consciously. By living in the present, we free ourselves from worries and anxieties about what could have been or what might come, and learn to appreciate what is.

Another essential aspect of spiritual awakening is connecting with oneself. In a world full of distractions, we often disconnect from our own essence. We spend so much time responding to the expectations of others or trying to fit into molds imposed by society that we forget who we really are. Spiritual awakening invites us to return to ourselves, to listen carefully to ourselves and to discover our true passions, desires and needs. As we get to know ourselves more deeply, we begin to make decisions that are more aligned with our authentic self, leading us to a fuller and more satisfying life.

Meditation, reflection, and introspection are powerful tools in this process. They allow us to observe our thoughts and emotions without judgment, which helps us to understand ourselves better and develop greater self-compassion. Rather than rejecting or avoiding aspects of ourselves that we consider negative, spiritual awakening teaches us to embrace all parts of our being, both the light and the dark. This leads to a deeper acceptance of ourselves and others, which fosters inner peace.

Furthermore, the path to spiritual awakening is not just about oneself. As we become more aware and connected to our inner selves, we also begin to see how we are connected to the world around us. We develop a sense of oneness with others, with nature, and with the universe as a whole. This sense of interconnectedness leads us to act more compassionately and caringly, as we understand that what we do to others we also do to ourselves. In this sense, spiritual awakening is not a selfish act, but a transformation that positively impacts the environment.

It is important to remember that spiritual awakening is not a final destination that is definitively reached, but rather an ongoing process of growth and learning. Along the way, there will be moments of clarity and peace, but also moments of doubt and discomfort. The crucial thing is not to rush or force the process. Each person has their own pace and their own lessons to learn. The spiritual path is not about achieving perfection, but about living more consciously and authentically, learning to enjoy the journey rather than always being focused on the destination.

In short, the path to spiritual awakening is a journey that begins with a desire to know oneself more deeply and to live a more authentic life. It is a process that invites us to question our beliefs, to detach ourselves from the superficial, and to connect with our purest essence. Through meditation, mindfulness, and introspection, we can learn to live more consciously and in harmony with ourselves and the world around us. Although the journey can be challenging at times, each step we take brings us closer to a life of peace, compassion, and fulfillment.

Connecting with the Inner Being

Connecting with the inner self is like embarking on a journey into the depths of oneself, a journey in which we slowly discover who we really are beyond the labels, roles and expectations that the world has imposed on us. In daily life, we are so immersed in our responsibilities, worries and the constant noise of the environment, that we often forget to pause and listen to that inner voice that guides us. That voice is none other than our inner self, that part of us that is always present, but that we often do not pay the attention it deserves.

When we talk about connecting with our inner self, we are referring to developing a closer relationship with ourselves. It is about learning to listen to ourselves without external distractions and to understand our deepest emotions, desires, fears and longings. Many times, we find it easier to listen to what others have to say about us than to stop and listen to what we really feel. This disconnection happens because we have grown up in a society that teaches us to look outside for validation, instead of looking inside.

The first step to connecting with the inner self is precisely learning to be silent. Not the external silence, but that internal silence that arises when we turn off the constant conversation of our mind, which is often filled with worries, to-do lists, and thoughts about the past or the future. To find this silence, meditation is a fundamental tool. It is not about doing something complicated, but about sitting in a quiet place and observing your breathing, thoughts, and sensations without judging them. At first it may seem difficult, as our mind is used to being in motion, but over time, we begin to experience a sense of calm and clarity.

Once we manage to be in that state of silence, that's when we can really start to hear what our inner self has to say. Sometimes, this voice is soft, almost imperceptible, and it may take us a while to recognize it. But the more we give ourselves the space to listen to it, the clearer it becomes. The inner self speaks to us through our emotions, our intuitions, and those sensations that we sometimes can't explain, but that we feel as an inner truth. It shows us what really makes us happy, what gives us peace, and what we need to feel fulfilled.

Another way to connect with the inner self is through introspection. This means taking an honest look at our beliefs, thoughts, and actions and asking ourselves if they are aligned with who we really are. Often, we act according to what we think we should do, rather than what we truly feel is right for us. We conform to the expectations of society, family, or work, not realizing that in the process, we are losing our essence. Introspection helps us identify these disconnections and correct course.

The inner self also manifests itself when we do activities that make us feel alive, connected, and at peace. For some people, this may be painting, writing, walking in nature, or simply spending time alone. These activities allow us to reconnect with who we really are, as they give us a sense of fulfillment and well-being. It is important to make time for what makes us feel in harmony, even if life constantly asks us to be busy. Connecting with the inner self is not a luxury, but a necessity to live an authentic and fulfilling life.

Once we begin to establish a connection with our inner self, we start to notice changes in the way we relate to the world. We become more aware of our decisions and begin to take actions that are more aligned with our deepest values and desires. Instead of acting out of obligation or fear of what others might think, we begin to act from a place of authenticity. This doesn't mean that life becomes perfect overnight, but it does mean that we begin to feel more at peace with our choices and more connected to the purpose that guides us.

Another key aspect of connecting with the inner self is learning to accept ourselves as we are. We live in a world that constantly pushes us to change, to improve, to be more successful, more attractive, more productive. But the inner self doesn't demand any of this. The inner self simply is, and when we acknowledge this, we realize that we don't need to be perfect to be valuable. Accepting our imperfections, our mistakes, and our weaknesses is part of the process of connecting with that deeper part of ourselves. In doing so, we develop a more compassionate relationship with ourselves, which in turn allows us to have more authentic and loving relationships with others.

The connection with the inner self is also nurtured when we learn to listen to our body. We often think of the body and mind as separate, but in reality, they are deeply interconnected. Our body is a reflection of our emotional and mental state. When we are stressed, worried, or disconnected from our inner self, our body reflects this through tension, tiredness, or even illness. Learning to listen to what our body tells us is a way to take care of our inner connection. Practicing relaxation exercises, yoga, or simply taking time to rest and nourish ourselves are ways to strengthen this bond.

Connecting with the inner self is an ongoing process that requires patience and dedication. It is not something that is achieved overnight, nor is it something that can be forced. But over time, we begin to notice how this connection brings us more clarity, peace, and meaning in life. We become more aware of our emotions and needs, and are able to live in a more authentic and fulfilling way. This process also helps us deal with life's challenges from a place of greater serenity, as we know that no matter what happens on the outside, we can always return to that inner space of calm and wisdom.

In short, connecting with the inner self is one of the keys to living a more authentic and fulfilling life. It is a process that invites us to stop, listen, and get to know ourselves in a deeper way. Through silence, introspection, and acceptance, we can develop a closer relationship with our essential self, allowing us to live in a way that is more aligned with our deepest values and desires. And while the path is not always easy, the benefits of this inner connection are immense, giving us a sense of peace and purpose that accompanies us every step of the way.

Developing Mindfulness

Developing mindfulness is like learning to be truly present in every moment of our lives. In the modern world, where everything seems to go so fast and distractions are constant, we often spend our days on autopilot, not really paying attention to what we are doing or feeling. We move from one task to another, our minds jumping between the past and the future, worrying about what we did or what will come, but we almost never stop to fully experience the here and now. Mindfulness is just that: learning to live in the present with full awareness, without letting thoughts drag us to other places.

One of the great benefits of mindfulness is that it allows us to experience life with more clarity and serenity. By practicing it, we begin to notice details that previously went unnoticed. Mindfulness is not just about being more focused, but about being more connected to what is happening in the moment, whether it is the sound of birds chirping when we wake up, the aroma of coffee in the morning, or the feeling of the air on our skin as we walk. These small daily experiences, which we often take for granted, can become sources of pleasure and tranquility when we give them full attention.

But mindfulness isn't just about being aware of what's going on around us. It also means being aware of what's going on inside us: our thoughts, emotions, and physical sensations. Normally, we live trapped in our thoughts, which go back and forth like a radio that never turns off. Without realizing it, our thoughts control us and lead us to react impulsively to situations. Developing mindfulness teaches us to observe those thoughts without judging them or getting carried away by them. It allows us to create a space between what we think and what we do, which helps us respond in a more conscious and less reactive way.

An easy way to start developing mindfulness is through breathing. Breathing is something that is always with us, and although it is an automatic function, we can use it as an anchor to bring us back to the present moment. A simple exercise is to sit in a quiet place and, for a few minutes, just focus on breathing. Feel the air entering through your nose, filling your lungs, and then slowly exiting. Whenever your mind wanders off, which is a natural thing to do, simply bring your attention back to your breathing. With practice, this simple act of observing your breathing helps you train your mind to be more present.

Mindfulness can also be practiced in any daily activity. You don't have to sit down and meditate to develop this skill. We can practice it while eating, for example. Instead of wolfing down food without thinking about what we're eating, as often happens, mindfulness invites us to savour each bite, to pay attention to the textures, flavours and aromas. We can also practice it when we walk, feeling the contact of our feet with the ground, noticing our surroundings, observing what's around us without getting caught up in distracting thoughts. The key is to return to the present time and time again.

At first, it may seem difficult. We are so used to being everywhere but in the present that our mind will resist. But with constant practice, we will find that it becomes easier and easier to return to the now. And the most interesting thing is that, by doing so, we begin to feel more peaceful. Stress and anxiety, which are often related to excessive thinking about the future or the past, begin to reduce. When we are fully present, there is no room for worry. We are simply here, experiencing life as it is.

Mindfulness also helps us develop a better relationship with our emotions. Normally, when we feel intense emotions, such as anger or sadness, we tend to react automatically, sometimes impulsively, without realizing what is really going on inside us. By practicing mindfulness, we learn to observe those emotions when they arise, without completely identifying with them. This doesn't mean that we stop feeling, but rather that we begin to see emotions for what they are: temporary responses that come and go, and not something that should define us. This simple observation allows us to have more control over how we respond to our emotions, rather than being carried away by them.

Another important aspect of mindfulness is that it teaches us not to judge what we experience. We live in a culture that pushes us to label everything as good or bad, pleasant or unpleasant. But mindfulness invites us to simply observe, without judgment. If we are having a bad day or feeling overwhelmed, instead of resisting or wanting to change what we feel immediately, mindfulness invites us to accept what is happening as it is. This doesn't mean resigning ourselves, but rather allowing ourselves to experience our emotions and thoughts without fighting them. When we stop resisting, negative emotions lose their strength and eventually dissipate.

Developing mindfulness also helps us cultivate greater gratitude. By being more present, we begin to notice and appreciate things that previously went unnoticed. We notice small, everyday miracles, like the warmth of the sun on our skin or the smile of a loved one. These moments, which might have previously seemed trivial, begin to take on new meaning. Gratitude arises naturally when we are more present, as we become aware of the abundance that already exists in our lives.

As we develop mindfulness, we also notice how our ability to concentrate improves. By being more present in the here and now, we are able to better focus on the tasks in front of us, which in turn increases our productivity and reduces mental exhaustion. Instead of jumping from one task to another or getting distracted by unnecessary thoughts, we learn to be completely present in what we are doing, which allows us to enjoy our activities more and perform them more effectively.

In short, developing mindfulness is a powerful tool that helps us live more consciously, connected and at peace. It is a process that requires practice and patience, but the benefits it brings are immense. It allows us to experience life in all its fullness, without getting caught up in the constant coming and going of thoughts. It teaches us to appreciate the present moment, to better manage our emotions and to live with more gratitude and serenity. Although modern life pushes us to always be busy, mindfulness reminds us that true wealth lies in being fully present in each moment, here and now.

Internal Silence

Inner silence is that deep calm that we can all find within ourselves when we turn off the constant noise of our mind. We live in a world full of noise, not only external, like traffic, music or conversations, but also within ourselves. Our mind is almost always busy, jumping from one thought to another, worrying about what happened yesterday or what might happen tomorrow. This constant chatter inside our heads keeps us distracted, away from ourselves and from the peace that we can find if we manage to silence that voice for a moment.

Finding inner silence isn't easy at first. For many, the very concept of "silence" can seem strange or unattainable. We're so used to always being busy, with our attention caught up in a thousand things at once, that the idea of stopping and just "being" seems unnatural. But it's precisely in that act of stopping, of letting go of distractions and worries, that we can begin to discover a new dimension of ourselves.

Inner silence does not refer to the complete absence of thoughts, as our mind will always produce thoughts naturally. Rather, it is about learning to observe those thoughts without getting carried away by them. It is like sitting by a river and watching the leaves float in the water without trying to catch them. Thoughts are like those leaves: they come and go, but we do not need to follow them. We can observe them without reacting. This gives us the necessary distance so that the noise of the mind does not control us.

A powerful way to begin cultivating inner silence is through meditation. Meditation is a practice that teaches us to be still, both physically and mentally. By sitting quietly and observing our breathing or any sensation in our body, we are training our mind to be quiet. At first, it can be frustrating because just when we try to be quiet, that's when the mental noise seems loudest. Thoughts about work, family, responsibilities—it all comes rushing in. But with patience and practice, little by little, our mind begins to calm down, and a space of silence begins to emerge.

This inner silence is not something we can only experience in moments of meditation. As we practice more, we begin to bring that state of calm and presence to other areas of our lives. We can be walking down the street, working, or talking to someone, and still feel that inner stillness. The noise outside is still there, but it no longer affects us in the same way. We have learned to find a refuge within ourselves, a space that is beyond external circumstances.

Inner silence also connects us to our intuition. Amidst the constant noise of the mind, we often lose touch with that inner voice that guides us most deeply. Intuition is a form of wisdom that emerges when we are calm, when we are not trying to figure everything out through logic or analysis. In silence, we begin to hear that small inner voice that knows what is right for us, even when our mind doesn't have all the answers. This intuition doesn't always come in the form of words; sometimes, it's just a feeling, a certainty felt in the body or heart.

Another aspect of inner silence is that it helps us to really know who we are. When we are constantly distracted or entertained, we never have time to reflect on our life, our choices, or our true desires. It is in those moments of silence that we can pause and ask: What do I really want? Am I living in accordance with my values? Inner silence offers us the space to ask ourselves these questions without rushing, without pressure, and to find answers that arise from deep within us.

Furthermore, inner silence has a transformative effect on how we handle stress and difficult emotions. When we are out of touch with that calm space within ourselves, emotions like anger, sadness, or anxiety easily overwhelm us. We react impulsively, letting ourselves be carried away by what we feel in the moment. But when we cultivate inner silence, we learn to respond to emotions rather than react. Instead of letting ourselves be swept away by anger or frustration, we can take a moment to breathe, connect with that inner stillness, and act from a place of greater clarity and control.

Inner silence also invites us to live in a simpler, more authentic way. In our everyday lives, we often feel pressured to do more, achieve more, be more. This constant external search can be exhausting. But when we begin to connect with inner silence, we realize that we don't need to do so much to be happy. Happiness and peace are not found in doing more, but in being more aware, in being more present in each moment. Silence teaches us to appreciate simplicity, to enjoy what we already have instead of always searching for something more.

An effective way to integrate inner silence into our daily lives is to create small moments of pause. We don't always need long meditation sessions to experience silence. We can find moments of silence when we wake up in the morning before the day begins, or when walking in nature, without the need to listen to music or talk. These moments of pause remind us that we always have access to that space of calm, no matter what is happening around us.

Inner silence also has an impact on our relationships. When we learn to be silent with ourselves, we become better listeners to others as well. Often in conversations, we are so busy thinking about what we are going to say next that we don't really hear what the other person is saying. Inner silence teaches us to listen fully, without rushing to respond. This creates a deeper connection with others as we give them our time and attention without distraction.

In conclusion, inner silence is a powerful tool to find peace, clarity, and authenticity in our lives. It is not something that is achieved overnight, but with practice, we can learn to quiet the mental noise and access that space of calm and wisdom that has always been within us. It is in that silence where we discover who we really are, where we find the answers we seek so much, and where we can live more fully and consciously. Inner silence is not a state of emptiness, but a space full of possibilities, where everything that really matters can emerge and flourish.

A Holistic Approach

A holistic approach is a way of seeing the world and ourselves in a whole, integrated way. The word "holistic" comes from the Greek word "holos," meaning "whole," and refers to the idea that we are more than the sum of our parts. Rather than looking at our lives in separate compartments—such as physical health, mind, emotions, spirit—a holistic approach recognizes that all of these parts are connected to one another. We cannot work on one aspect of ourselves without affecting the others. In fact, when we take our whole selves into account, we achieve a more balanced, fulfilled, and authentic life.

This approach is especially important when we talk about our overall well-being and, in the context of spiritual psychology, it plays a crucial role in our personal and spiritual growth. Often, modern life pushes us to focus solely on certain aspects, such as work or material success, leaving aside our emotions, relationships or spirituality. We focus so much on the external that we forget what is going on inside us. A holistic approach invites us to stop and look at each area of our life with equal importance, as the well-being of one inevitably affects the well-being of the others.

For example, if we only care about our physical health and strive to eat well and exercise, but we don't pay attention to our mental or emotional health, we'll soon notice an imbalance. Perhaps our body is in good shape, but if we're emotionally drained or stressed, our overall health will suffer. Likewise, if we focus too much on our work life and neglect our personal relationships, we can feel disconnected, even if we're achieving professional success. A holistic approach reminds us that true well-being comes from taking care of every part of our life in a balanced way.

By taking a holistic approach, we not only improve our physical or mental health, but we also nourish our spiritual life. Spirituality, in this context, does not necessarily refer to religion, but to that deeper sense of connection with ourselves and something greater than ourselves. Whether we call it the universe, nature, or simply higher consciousness, this connection is critical to feeling whole. When we disconnect from this aspect of our life, we often feel a void that we cannot fill with external achievements.

Part of the holistic approach is realizing that our body, mind, and spirit are deeply interconnected. If we are going through an emotionally difficult time, we may also experience physical symptoms, such as headaches, fatigue, or digestive issues. Likewise, when we take care of our body through healthy eating, exercise, and adequate rest, our mind feels clearer and our emotions are more stable. We cannot separate these parts of ourselves, as they all form a single, intertwined whole.

A holistic approach also involves paying attention to our relationships with others. As humans, we are social by nature and our connections with others are essential to our well-being. However, in everyday life, we often take our relationships for granted or get caught up in the stresses and strains of life, which affects the quality of our interactions. The holistic approach encourages us to cultivate healthy and meaningful relationships as these are also integral to our overall well-being. The way we relate to others directly affects our emotional and mental health, and also our spirituality, as through our connections with others we can find a deeper sense of purpose and belonging.

In addition to our personal relationships, a holistic approach also extends to our relationship with our environment. Nature is a powerful source of balance and healing, and when we connect with it, we can feel a deep sense of peace and well-being. Walking through the woods, feeling the wind on our skin, or listening to the sound of running water can have a rejuvenating effect on our mind and spirit. However, in modern life, we often find ourselves disconnected from nature, spending most of our time in urban environments or in front of screens. A holistic approach invites us to reconnect with nature and recognize the importance of caring for the environment, as our well-being and the well-being of the planet are intimately linked.

Another key aspect of the holistic approach is awareness of our thoughts and beliefs. Often, limiting beliefs or negative thoughts can have a profound impact on our lives. For example, if we believe that we are not good enough or that we do not deserve success, these beliefs will affect how we feel and act, even on a physical level. The holistic approach teaches us to be aware of these thought patterns and work to transform them into more positive and constructive beliefs. In this way, we can begin to create a life that is more aligned with our true desires and aspirations.

A holistic approach also values the importance of introspection and self-knowledge. By taking the time to reflect on our life, our actions, and our emotions, we begin to know ourselves better. This self-knowledge is essential for our personal and spiritual growth, as only when we are aware of our strengths and weaknesses, our fears and desires, can we begin to make the changes necessary to live more authentically. Introspection is not just about looking inward, but also about taking action based on what we discover about ourselves.

Finally, a holistic approach invites us to live with intention. This means being aware of our daily choices and making sure they are aligned with our values and goals. Living with intention doesn't mean that we always have all the answers or that our life is perfect, but rather that we are committed to living in a way that reflects who we are at our core. It's about making conscious choices rather than being carried away by circumstances or the frenetic pace of life.

In short, a holistic approach is a path to a more balanced, conscious, and fulfilling life. It reminds us that we cannot separate our different facets—physical, mental, emotional, spiritual—and that by taking care of all of them, we create a more harmonious and meaningful life. This approach teaches us to pay attention to all areas of our lives, from our personal relationships to our connection to nature, and to live with greater awareness and intention. By taking a holistic approach, we begin to see life not as a series of isolated tasks and challenges, but as a complete, integrated experience, full of opportunities to grow, learn, and flourish.

Breaking the Chains of the Ego

Breaking the chains of ego is an essential process on the path to personal growth and spiritual awakening. Ego, as we understand it in this context, does not simply refer to self-esteem or self-confidence, but to that part of our mind that is obsessed with image, control, recognition, and attachment to material things. It is that inner voice that tells us we must be better than others, have more success, more wealth, or more power. The ego is constantly seeking external validation, and many times, it distances us from who we really are.

The ego is like an invisible prison we build around ourselves. It makes us believe that we are only worth what we have or what we achieve. It drives us to compare ourselves to others, to live in a constant state of competition, and to measure our success through superficial parameters. When we are trapped in the ego, our happiness depends on external factors: whether we receive enough recognition, whether we achieve what we want, whether others see us in a certain way. But what happens when we don't get what we want? The ego leaves us in an endless cycle of dissatisfaction, always chasing something that never fully fulfills us.

One of the main problems with the ego is that it disconnects us from our deeper self. By focusing so much on how others see us, on what we think we should have or be, we stop listening to our true inner voice. The ego creates a barrier between us and our most authentic essence, that part of us that is at peace, that doesn't need to compete, that doesn't need validation from anyone. The ego keeps us trapped on the surface of life, while our essence is searching for something deeper, something more real.

Breaking the chains of ego doesn't mean we stop being ourselves, or abandon our goals or dreams. Rather, it's about freeing ourselves from the need for our identity to be tied to those achievements. It's about learning to let go of attachment to what the outside world expects of us and start living from a place of authenticity and truth. When we break the chains of ego, we begin to see life in a different way. We realize that we don't need to be constantly striving for recognition or approval from others. We can be happy and feel at peace no matter what the external circumstances are.

One of the first steps in breaking free from the ego is recognizing that we are not our thoughts. The ego is largely a mental construct. It tells us stories about who we are and what our lives should be like, but those stories are not the absolute truth. They are just narratives we have created or absorbed from our environment. When we identify too closely with those stories, we become prisoners of them. But when we realize that we can observe those thoughts without fully believing them, we begin to dismantle the ego's power over us.

The practice of meditation and mindfulness are powerful tools for freeing ourselves from ego. By meditating, we learn to observe our thoughts and emotions without identifying with them. This allows us to see more clearly how the ego operates in our daily lives. We may notice how the ego reacts when we feel criticized or when someone doesn't give us the recognition we think we deserve. Or we may notice how the ego drives us to judge others in order to feel superior. By becoming aware of these patterns, we can slowly begin to let go of them.

Another key aspect of breaking the chains of ego is learning to let go of control. The ego always wants to be in control of everything: our circumstances, the people around us, even the future. It makes us believe that if we control enough, we will be happy. But the truth is that control is an illusion. Life is uncertain and there will always be things that are beyond our control. When we accept this reality and learn to flow with the changes, the ego loses its power. Instead of resisting what we cannot change, we learn to adapt and find peace in the process.

Detachment is another important step in this process. The ego attaches itself to external things—possessions, titles, status, relationships—and when we lose any of these things, we feel devastated. But when we begin to detach, it doesn't mean we stop valuing what we have or the people in our lives. Rather, it means we stop basing our identity on them. We understand that everything in life is temporary and that our true worth is not dependent on what we possess or achieve. This frees us to live more authentically and without fear of loss.

Breaking the chains of ego also allows us to see others in a more compassionate way. Ego drives us to see others as competitors, as obstacles we need to overcome. It makes us feel envious when someone has something we want or makes us judge people who are different from us. But when we start to let go of ego, we realize that we are all on the same journey. We are all dealing with our own internal struggles. Instead of competing or comparing ourselves, we can begin to feel empathy and compassion for others. This improves our relationships and helps us connect in a more genuine way.

It is also important to mention that the process of breaking away from the ego does not happen overnight. It is an ongoing work, and there will be times when the ego takes over again. But the most important thing is to be aware of those moments and get back on track. Every time we choose not to react from the ego, we are taking a step closer to our freedom. It is a journey of self-discovery and transformation that brings us closer to our true essence.

Ultimately, breaking the chains of ego frees us to live a fuller, more meaningful life. It allows us to experience life from a place of peace and authenticity, without being caught up in the constant need for external validation. When we let go of ego, we discover that we don't need to be someone else or have more to feel complete. We are already enough just as we are. This realization opens the door to a life that is simpler, more loving, and more connected to the world around us.

In short, the ego is a part of us that seeks control, validation and recognition, but when we let it rule our lives, it disconnects us from our true essence. Breaking the chains of the ego involves recognizing its influence, letting go of control, practicing detachment and cultivating awareness of our thoughts and emotions. It is an ongoing process that leads us to a freer, more authentic life at peace with ourselves and with others.

The Awakening of Consciousness

The awakening of consciousness is one of the most profound and transformative processes that we can experience as human beings. It is an internal change in the way we perceive the world and ourselves. This awakening does not happen suddenly or by chance; it is a gradual process that occurs when we begin to question our beliefs, our thought patterns, and our way of relating to life. It is when we stop living on autopilot and begin to be fully aware of each of our actions, thoughts, and emotions.

For most of our lives, we live trapped in a daily routine that disconnects us from our essence. We let ourselves be carried away by stress, worries, and habits that we have acquired over time. Many times, we don't even realize that we are acting mechanically, repeating patterns without stopping to question them. The awakening of consciousness invites us to stop, to look at our lives from another perspective, and to start living with more intention and purpose.

An awakening of consciousness begins with the ability to observe ourselves. It is learning to witness our thoughts, emotions, and actions without reacting automatically. Instead of being carried away by our emotions or impulses, we begin to ask ourselves why we feel a certain way or why we react to certain situations in a repetitive way. This type of observation allows us to clearly see the patterns we have accumulated, many of which can be limiting or destructive. Through this self-observation, we realize that we are more than our thoughts or emotions. There is a part of us that is able to observe everything without identifying with it.

This process of awakening is not always easy. Sometimes it can be uncomfortable to realize that we have been living in a way that does not satisfy us or that does not reflect who we really are. But it is precisely in those moments of discomfort that we begin to grow. Awakening consciousness involves breaking old habits, unlearning limiting beliefs, and beginning to create a new reality based on our inner truth. This requires courage and a willingness to change.

One of the first steps in awakening consciousness is realizing that many of the beliefs we have about ourselves and the world are not necessarily true. Often, we have adopted beliefs that come from our family, our culture, or our past experiences, without ever questioning them. These beliefs can influence how we view life and how we behave. For example, if we believe that success is only measured in terms of money or status, we may spend our lives pursuing these goals, not realizing that they do not actually make us feel complete. By awakening our consciousness, we begin to question these beliefs and search for what truly gives us meaning and purpose.

Awakening consciousness also involves being more present in the moment. More often than not, our minds are stuck in the past or worried about the future. We lament over things that have already happened or worry about what might happen, and in that process, we lose sight of the present. But the only moment we really have is now. Being present means paying attention to what we are doing right now, whether it is something as simple as washing the dishes or chatting with a friend. When we are fully present, we experience life in a deeper, more meaningful way.

Part of awakening consciousness is realizing that we are not separate from the world around us. Often, the ego makes us feel like we are isolated, that we are individuals separate from others. But when our consciousness awakens, we begin to see the connections between ourselves and the universe. We realize that we are part of something much bigger, and that our actions, thoughts, and emotions have an impact on everything around us. This understanding leads us to act with more compassion, not only towards ourselves, but also towards others and the environment. We become more aware of how our decisions affect others, and we begin to make decisions that are more aligned with the well-being of all.

Another important aspect of awakening consciousness is learning to let go of attachment to the outcome. We often live with the expectation that things must happen in a specific way for us to be happy. We become attached to certain outcomes and when we don't get them, we suffer. Awakening consciousness teaches us to accept life as it is, to flow with what happens, rather than fighting against it. This doesn't mean that we stop having goals or desires, but that we learn to let go of the outcome and trust that everything unfolds as it should.

Once we begin to awaken our consciousness, we also realize the importance of taking care of our mind and body. These two aspects are deeply connected. If our mind is filled with negative or toxic thoughts, this can affect our physical health, and vice versa. By awakening our consciousness, we become more responsible for our well-being. We begin to make more conscious choices regarding what we eat, how we treat our body, and how we handle our emotions. Taking care of our physical and mental health becomes an integral part of our spiritual growth.

The awakening of consciousness is also a process of self-discovery. As we become more conscious, we begin to discover who we really are, beyond the masks we have built over time. We realize that we are not simply the role we play in society, such as mother, father, professional, or friend. We are much more complex and deeper beings, with desires, passions, and a purpose that goes beyond what society has taught us. This process of self-discovery can be liberating, as it allows us to live in a more authentic way and aligned with our true nature.

On this journey towards awakening consciousness, it is essential to practice gratitude. Often, we are so focused on what we lack or what we have not achieved, that we forget about everything we already have. Practicing gratitude helps us to change our perspective and realize that, regardless of our circumstances, there is always something to be grateful for. This simple act of giving thanks connects us to the present and fills us with a sense of fulfillment and satisfaction.

Awakening consciousness is an ongoing process. It is not something that happens overnight, nor is it something that is achieved once and for all. It is a path in which we continue to learn, grow, and deepen our connection with ourselves and the world. As we continue to awaken, we discover new layers of our consciousness, new ways of seeing life, and new ways of being. It is a never-ending journey, but each step we take brings us closer to our truth and allows us to live more fully and consciously.

In short, the awakening of consciousness is a process of self-discovery and transformation that invites us to live with greater presence, authenticity and purpose. It is about learning to observe our thoughts, to question our beliefs and to be more present in the moment. It connects us with our true essence and frees us from the limiting patterns that we have accumulated throughout our lives. By awakening our consciousness, we begin to see the world in a deeper and more meaningful way, and to live with more peace and harmony, both with ourselves and with our environment.

61

Healing the Spirit

Healing the spirit is a deeply personal and transformative process. Throughout our lives, we accumulate wounds that, although often not visible to the naked eye, can leave us with emotional and spiritual scars. These wounds can come from difficult experiences, traumas, failed relationships, moments of sadness, or simply from the feeling of disconnection with ourselves and the world. The spirit, that deepest and most essential part of who we are, is sometimes neglected or forgotten amidst the hustle and bustle of everyday life. Healing the spirit means reconnecting with that essential part of our being, giving it the care and attention it needs to restore balance and inner peace.

The first step in the spiritual healing process is to recognize that just like the body or mind, the spirit can also be hurt. We often live our lives trying to ignore the signs that something inside us needs to be taken care of. We get distracted by work, social media, daily activities, and we neglect the time needed to look inward. However, the spirit sends us signals when it needs to be healed. It can manifest in feelings of emptiness, disconnection, deep sadness, or a sense of being lost without a clear purpose. Paying attention to these signs is the first clue that we need to do something about it.

One of the most powerful ways to heal the spirit is through forgiveness. Many of our spiritual wounds come from situations where we have been hurt by others or where we have failed ourselves. Resentment and guilt are weights we carry that keep us from moving forward. Forgiveness is not only an act toward others, but also toward ourselves. Forgiveness does not mean forgetting or justifying what was done to us, but rather freeing ourselves from the power those wounds have over us. It means saying, "I'm not going to let this control my life anymore," and opening our hearts to the possibility of healing and moving forward. Forgiveness gives us the freedom to let go of the pain and allow our spirit to heal.

Another key aspect of spiritual healing is self-care. Taking care of our spirit means nourishing it with what makes us feel connected, alive, and at peace. This can vary from person to person: for some, it may be spending time in nature, meditating, or practicing silence. For others, it may mean reconnecting with creativity, painting, writing, or playing music. The important thing is to identify those activities that make us feel fulfilled and dedicate time to them in our daily routine. These are not just superficial activities, but those that allow us to be in touch with the deepest part of our being, with who we really are.

Meditation and introspection also play an important role in spiritual healing. Often, we live our lives so busy that we don't take the time to be quiet with ourselves. Meditation allows us to create a space where we can observe our thoughts and emotions without judging them. It helps us to calm the mind and get in touch with our spirit, to listen to that inner voice that is often drowned out by the noise outside. Through meditation, we can access a source of peace and clarity that resides deep within us, and from there, begin to heal.

Healing the spirit also involves letting go of control. Spiritual suffering often comes from our struggle to control every aspect of our lives. We want things to go a certain way, we want people to behave a certain way, and when they don't, we feel frustration and pain. Learning to let go of control means accepting that we cannot have control over everything, and that it's okay to do so. Life has its own flow, and when we learn to trust the process, rather than fight it, we find greater inner peace. Letting go of control is not giving up, but flowing with life in a wiser, more conscious way.

In addition to letting go of control, it is essential to practice detachment. Many times, spiritual wounds come from our attachment to things, people, or situations that no longer serve us, but which we hold on to out of fear of change or loss. Detachment does not mean that we do not value what we have, but rather that we understand that nothing is permanent. Relationships, experiences, even our own bodies, are transitory. Practicing detachment allows us to accept the changing nature of life without desperately clinging to what will inevitably change or disappear. This act of letting go frees our spirit and gives us the ability to live more fully in the present.

Another important part of the spiritual healing process is cultivating gratitude. Often, our spiritual wounds are exacerbated because we focus on what we lack or what went wrong in our lives. But when we begin to practice gratitude, we change our perspective. We begin to notice all the blessings we have, the little things we often overlook but that are fundamental to our happiness. Gratitude connects us to the abundance of the present moment and reminds us that despite difficulties, there is always something to be grateful for. This shift in focus helps us heal our spirit, as it takes us away from pain and brings us closer to inner peace.

Part of healing the spirit also involves learning to let go of the past. We often carry the weight of our past experiences, the mistakes we have made, or decisions that did not turn out the way we expected. The past can become a heavy burden that prevents us from moving forward. Healing means freeing ourselves from that weight, learning from our experiences, and letting go of what no longer serves us. We cannot change what has already happened, but we can change how we relate to those experiences. Instead of seeing them as failures, we can see them as opportunities for growth and learning.

Self-love is also an essential component of spiritual healing. Many times, our spiritual wounds come from a lack of love and compassion for ourselves. We judge ourselves harshly, punish ourselves for our mistakes, and deny ourselves the care we need. Healing the spirit means learning to treat ourselves kindly, to accept ourselves as we are, with our virtues and flaws. Self-love allows us to recognize that we are worthy of happiness, peace, and living a full life. When we cultivate self-love, our spirit begins to heal naturally.

Finally, healing the spirit is an ongoing process. It is not something that happens overnight, nor is it a goal that we achieve once and for all. Like the body and mind, the spirit requires constant attention. There will be times when we feel more connected and at peace, and other times when we feel pain or disconnection again. The important thing to remember is that we can always come back to ourselves, that we can always get back on the path of healing, no matter how many times we stray. Healing the spirit is a lifelong journey, but one that leads us to live with greater awareness, peace, and fulfillment.

Compassion and Self-Love

Compassion and self-love are two fundamental pillars for our emotional and spiritual well-being. Often in our day-to-day lives, we focus on others, on how we can help, care, and be present for the people around us. This, while a beautiful expression of our humanity, can leave out something equally important: how we treat ourselves. In order to authentically love and care for others, we first need to learn to treat ourselves with the same compassion and love we offer to others. It is not selfish to prioritize our well-being; it is necessary to live a full and balanced life.

Self-compassion is the act of being kind and understanding of our own imperfections. We all make mistakes, we all have moments of weakness, and that's okay. But often, when we're faced with our own mistakes, we're extremely harsh and critical of ourselves. We say things like "I should have done better" or "I'm a failure." These thoughts affect us deeply, undermining our self-esteem and well-being. Compassion, on the other hand, invites us to change that internal dialogue and treat ourselves with the same kindness we would show a close friend. If a friend told us they made a mistake, we wouldn't punish them or make them feel worse, right? So why do we do it to ourselves?

The first step in cultivating compassion is learning to acknowledge our thoughts and emotions without judging them. This means allowing ourselves to feel what we feel without punishing ourselves for it. If we are sad, angry, or frustrated, instead of judging those emotions as bad, we can accept them as part of our human experience. Being compassionate with ourselves means understanding that it is normal to feel bad sometimes, that we don't always have to be okay or have all the answers. By accepting our emotions as they are, we create a safe space for our emotional well-being.

Self-love, on the other hand, is the ability to value ourselves, without relying on external validation. We often look to others to value, acknowledge, or love us in order to feel good about who we are. But self-love teaches us that we don't need that external approval to feel complete. Self-love is not narcissism or arrogance, but an honest recognition of our worth as human beings. It means being aware of our strengths and weaknesses, and still loving ourselves completely. This doesn't mean that we ignore our areas for improvement, but that we allow ourselves to work on them from a place of love and not constant criticism.

One of the keys to cultivating self-love is learning to set healthy boundaries. Often, out of fear of rejection or conflict, we let others treat us in ways that hurt us. We allow other people to invade our personal or emotional space, and this can wear down our self-esteem. Setting boundaries means saying "no" when something doesn't make us feel good or when we need to take care of ourselves. These boundaries not only protect us, but they also send a clear message that we value ourselves and deserve respect. Learning to set boundaries is one of the most powerful ways to practice self-love, as it teaches us to prioritize our well-being without feeling guilty about it.

In addition to boundaries, another way to cultivate self-love is to make time for our needs. In a world that values productivity and efficiency, we often forget to take care of our body, mind, and spirit. We tell ourselves that we don't have time to rest, to do something we enjoy, or to simply unwind. However, self-love involves giving ourselves permission to enjoy activities that nourish us, that make us feel good and at peace. It can be something as simple as reading a book, going for a walk, meditating, or even taking a relaxing bath. These small actions not only recharge our energies, but they also send us a clear message: "I deserve this time for myself."

Compassion and self-love are also deeply connected to acceptance. Many times, our suffering comes from the fact that we don't accept who we are in the present moment. We want to be different, to change our circumstances, or to have a life that doesn't look like ours. This constant struggle to be "better" or "different" prevents us from seeing the beauty of who we already are. Acceptance doesn't mean conforming, but rather recognizing that, in this moment, we are enough just as we are. It allows us to embrace our imperfections, our flaws, and our quirks, and see them as part of what makes us unique. Accepting ourselves frees us from the pressure of being perfect and allows us to live more lightly and joyfully.

Part of compassion and self-love also involves learning to let go of the unrealistic expectations we have for ourselves. We live in a society that often demands that we always be successful, productive, and happy. We are bombarded with images of people who seem to have it all, which can make us feel like we are never good enough. But the truth is, no one is perfect, and we are all on a journey of growth and learning. By letting go of these expectations, we allow ourselves to be human, make mistakes, and move forward without beating ourselves up for not meeting those unattainable standards.

An essential component of self-love is also forgiveness. Throughout our lives, we inevitably make mistakes, making decisions that don't always turn out for the best. Yet, we often hold on to those mistakes, repeatedly punishing ourselves for what we did or didn't do. Forgiveness, both toward others and toward ourselves, is a liberating act that allows us to let go of the past and move forward. When we forgive ourselves, we are recognizing that we are constantly evolving human beings and that every experience, even painful ones, provides us with an opportunity to learn and grow.

Furthermore, compassion and self-love are not just something we practice internally; they also impact our relationships with others. When we are compassionate and loving toward ourselves, it is easier to extend that same compassion to the people around us. We no longer seek external validation to feel good, which allows us to relate to others from a place of authenticity and generosity. We don't need people to make us feel whole because we have already found that wholeness within ourselves. This transforms our relationships, making them healthier and more balanced.

Finally, self-love and compassion are not something that is achieved overnight. They are daily practices, small gestures of kindness towards ourselves that, over time, help us build a solid foundation of emotional and spiritual well-being. There will be days when it will be easier to be compassionate and others when it will be more difficult. The important thing to remember is that we can always return to ourselves, that we can always start over, no matter how many times we stray from the path. Practicing compassion and self-love is an ongoing journey, but it is one worth undertaking, because it leads us to live with more peace, joy and fulfillment.

In short, compassion and self-love are acts of care and respect towards ourselves. They are the recognition that, just like everyone else, we deserve to be treated with kindness, respect and love. By learning to treat ourselves with compassion, set boundaries, accept our imperfections and let go of unrealistic expectations, we free ourselves from the constant pressure to be perfect and begin to live a more authentic and meaningful life. Compassion and self-love allow us to heal, grow and connect with the best in ourselves, giving us the opportunity to live from a place of inner peace and deep well-being.

From Suffering to Enlightenment

Suffering is an experience we all experience at some point in our lives. It can be a loss, a disappointment, a betrayal, or simply the feeling that life is not turning out the way we expected. We often try to avoid suffering at all costs, looking for quick fixes or distractions that will take us away from that pain. However, what we don't always understand is that suffering has a deeper purpose and can be the catalyst for a spiritual awakening, a transformation that takes us from darkness to light, from confusion to clarity, and from pain to inner peace.

Most of us tend to think of suffering as something negative, something we should avoid or eliminate from our lives as quickly as possible. And in a sense, it's natural to want to run away from pain. After all, suffering makes us feel vulnerable, confronts us with our limitations, and can make us doubt ourselves and life itself. But what we don't often consider is that suffering has the power to teach us valuable lessons that we wouldn't learn otherwise. It's in the most difficult times that we often find the greatest opportunities for personal and spiritual growth.

When we are suffering, our initial tendency is to resist. We ask ourselves "why me?" or "why does it have to be so hard?" These kinds of questions are natural, but they often trap us in a cycle of ongoing pain. Resisting suffering, rather than facing it, only prolongs our agony. By resisting what we are experiencing, we deny the possibility of learning from it. Instead, when we accept suffering as part of life, we open the door to profound transformation. Acceptance does not mean resignation, but understanding that pain is an inevitable part of human existence, and that it can also be a powerful tool for our development.

One of the first steps to transforming suffering into enlightenment is to observe it without judging it. This may seem difficult at first, because when we are in the midst of pain, we tend to want to escape or find a quick fix. However, the key is to stop for a moment and allow ourselves to feel that pain in its entirety, without running away from it. In doing so, we begin to understand that suffering is not something external that attacks us, but rather an internal experience that we can observe and learn to manage. This observation, done from a place of full awareness, allows us to create a distance between ourselves and the suffering, giving us the space needed to see things more clearly.

Another important aspect of transforming suffering is changing our relationship to it. Instead of seeing it as a punishment or an injustice, we can begin to see it as an opportunity for growth. Life, by its nature, is not always easy. There will be moments of pain, of uncertainty, of fear. However, each of these moments can teach us something valuable if we are willing to listen. Sometimes, suffering shows us aspects of ourselves that we had ignored or repressed. It invites us to reflect on our decisions, our thought patterns, and our beliefs. Instead of focusing solely on the pain, we can ask ourselves, "What is this experience teaching me? What can I learn from this difficult time?"

This shift in perspective can be transformative. When we begin to see suffering as a teacher, rather than an enemy, we realize that we have the power to decide how we react to it. We can't control everything that happens to us in life, but we can control how we respond to those experiences. We can choose to resist, blame others, or victimize ourselves, or we can choose to face suffering courageously, learn from it, and allow it to transform us into more conscious and compassionate people.

It is important to understand that the path from suffering to enlightenment is not a linear process. There will be days when we feel lost, frustrated, and perhaps even hopeless. However, each of those moments is part of the process. It is through those ups and downs that we learn to find our true inner strength. As we face our shadows and accept our pain, we also discover the light that has always been within us, waiting to be revealed. That light is our true essence, our connection to something greater than ourselves.

Spirituality often invites us to look beyond external circumstances and focus on what is happening within us. When we suffer, we tend to look outside for answers or blame, but true transformation happens when we turn our gaze inward. What is this suffering telling us about our expectations, our beliefs, or our attachments? Many times, suffering arises when we cling to something that no longer serves us, when we have expectations that don't match reality, or when we resist the inevitable changes in life. By letting go of those attachments and expectations, we begin to free ourselves from suffering.

Detachment is a crucial lesson on the path to enlightenment. It doesn't mean we stop caring or having desires, but rather we learn not to depend on external outcomes for our happiness. When we are attached to certain expectations or outcomes, any deviation from that plan causes us suffering. By learning to let go and accept the uncertainty of life, we find an inner peace that is not tied to external circumstances. This peace is the first step toward enlightenment, a sense of calm that is not affected by the ups and downs of the outside world.

Enlightenment is not a destination that we reach, but rather a state of being that we access when we are fully present in the here and now. Many people think that enlightenment is something reserved for a select few, but in reality, it is accessible to everyone. It is about living in harmony with ourselves and the world around us, being aware of our actions, thoughts, and emotions, and acting from a place of love and compassion. Suffering, when handled wisely, can be the path that leads us to that higher state of consciousness.

Ultimately, the journey from suffering to enlightenment is a deeply personal process. There is no single path or magic formula. Each person will have their own experience and their own pace. The important thing to remember is that even in the darkest of times, there is always a light at the end of the tunnel. That light is not outside of us, but within. And each step we take toward that light brings us closer to our true essence, to peace, and to a deeper understanding of who we are and our place in the universe.

In conclusion, suffering is not something we should fear or avoid at all costs. If we face it with courage and a learning attitude, we can transform it into a powerful tool for our spiritual growth. Through suffering, we can learn to let go of our attachments, change our perspective, and find an inner peace that goes beyond external circumstances. This process leads us to enlightenment, a deeper understanding of life, and a more authentic connection with ourselves and the world around us.

The Art of Letting Go

Letting go is a seemingly simple act, but profoundly transformative in practice. We often hold on to things, people, ideas, beliefs, and expectations that no longer serve us, sometimes without even realizing it. We hold on because we believe that by maintaining control or security over certain parts of our lives, we will avoid pain or uncertainty. However, that need to hold on is often what ends up causing the most suffering. Learning to let go is, in essence, learning to live at peace with what is, accepting reality as it is, without resistance or struggle.

The first step to letting go is recognizing what we are holding on to. Many times we are not aware of our attachments. Perhaps we are holding on to a relationship that no longer makes us happy, or a job that drains us, or even a version of ourselves that no longer aligns with who we are in the present. To let go, we must first pause and look honestly at our lives. Where are we putting up resistance? What are we trying to control? This self-observation takes courage, because it can be uncomfortable to see the areas where we are attached to something that no longer serves us. However, this clarity is the first step toward liberation.

Letting go doesn't mean giving up or giving in. We often confuse the act of letting go with the idea that we're abandoning our desires or giving in to inertia. But letting go isn't passivity. In fact, it's a deeply active and conscious action. Letting go is a deliberate decision to release what is no longer aligned with our well-being, in order to open ourselves up to new opportunities and experiences. When we let go, we allow life to flow more naturally, without the barriers and obstacles we create when we try to control everything around us.

One of the biggest obstacles to letting go is fear. We are terrified of the idea of losing control. We think that if we let go of something, whether it be a situation or a person, we will lose something valuable. The fear of change and the unknown makes us cling even more to the familiar, even when that familiar thing is causing us harm. We stay in toxic relationships, in unfulfilling jobs, in self-destructive patterns of behavior, because the fear of what might happen if we let go paralyzes us. But in reality, fear is an illusion. When we finally dare to let go, we discover that what awaits us on the other side of fear is, almost always, more freedom, more peace, and more happiness.

The art of letting go involves trusting life. Trusting that even though we can't control every detail or outcome, life has a way of adjusting itself. When we let go, we stop trying to force things to happen a specific way. Instead, we learn to flow with what comes, to adapt to changes gracefully. This doesn't mean we don't have goals or aspirations, but rather that we don't get attached to "how" or "when" they will happen. Letting go frees us from the burden of perfection and allows us to enjoy the journey more, rather than constantly worrying about the final destination.

Another crucial aspect of letting go is emotional detachment. It doesn't mean that we stop feeling or that we become cold and indifferent. On the contrary, letting go allows us to experience emotions more fully, without getting stuck in them. When we hold on to an emotion, whether positive or negative, we limit our ability to live in the present. We hold on to moments of joy, wishing they would never end, or we hold on to pain, reliving it over and over again. But life is a constant flow of emotions and experiences. Nothing is permanent. By letting go, we allow ourselves to feel without getting stuck, knowing that every emotion, every experience, has its time and place, and that it, too, will eventually pass.

One of the most challenging times to let go is when we are faced with loss. It may be the loss of a loved one, a relationship, or an important stage in our lives. In these times, letting go can feel impossible. We cling to the past, to what was, because the pain of loss is overwhelming. However, learning to let go in these moments does not mean forgetting or minimizing what we have lost. It means accepting that everything in life is transitory. What we have lost will always have a place in our hearts, but we must also allow ourselves to move on. Letting go allows us to honor what was, while embracing what is and what is to come.

The practice of letting go is not something that happens overnight. It is an ongoing process that requires patience and compassion for ourselves. There will be times when we let go with ease and other times when the attachment will be stronger. The important thing to remember is that letting go is an act of self-love. By releasing what no longer serves us, we are allowing ourselves to grow, evolve, and move to a place of greater peace and clarity.

Letting go also allows us to be more present in the current moment. When we hold on to the past or our expectations about the future, we disconnect from the here and now. By letting go, we free ourselves from the chains of what is no longer there or what has not yet arrived. We learn to enjoy the present more, to appreciate the little things, and to be at peace with what is, rather than wishing for what was or what could be.

Ultimately, the art of letting go is a practice of freedom. It is letting go of what we cannot control, in order to focus on what we can: our attitude, our actions, and our ability to adapt to life's changes. Letting go frees us from unnecessary suffering and allows us to experience life in a more authentic and fulfilling way. It opens the doors to new possibilities and allows us to live from a place of trust and acceptance.

In short, letting go is one of the most valuable lessons we can learn on our path of personal and spiritual growth. It teaches us to trust, accept, and flow with life rather than resist it. It reminds us that true peace comes not from controlling everything around us, but from learning to let go of what we cannot change, and finding our strength and serenity in the midst of that process. Letting go is, at its core, an art, and by mastering it, we free ourselves to live a fuller, more present life, more in harmony with ourselves and the world around us.

Listening to the Soul through the Body

Our body is much more than a set of organs and bones that allow us to move and perform daily activities. The body is a vehicle that not only supports us, but is also a channel through which our soul expresses itself and communicates with us. We often think of the body and soul as separate entities, but they are actually deeply interconnected. Listening to the soul through the body is a skill that allows us to delve deeper into our being, understand what we truly need, and ultimately live a life more aligned with our true essence.

The body has an innate wisdom that goes beyond what we usually recognize. Have you ever felt a knot in your stomach before making an important decision, or a weight on your chest when something is not right? These are examples of how the body speaks to us, showing us through physical sensations what our words and thoughts sometimes fail to express. The soul, through the body, sends signals that we can interpret if we pay attention. These physical sensations are not just meaningless discomforts or annoyances; they are deep messages that invite us to pay attention to what is happening inside us.

Listening to the soul through the body requires us to slow down and cultivate mindfulness. In modern life, we are constantly bombarded by external stimuli, which leads us to disconnect from our own body. We find ourselves more focused on the screens of our phones or computers, on the endless daily tasks, and less on what is happening inside us. When we are not in tune with our body, we lose the ability to listen to the subtle signals it sends us. Therefore, it is essential that we learn to create spaces of calm and stillness in our life to reconnect with our body and, through it, with our soul.

One of the simplest and most effective ways to begin listening to the soul through the body is to pay attention to the breath. Breathing is the bridge between the body and the soul. It is an automatic process, but it is also something we can consciously control. By observing our breathing, we begin to tune into the state of our body and mind. Rapid, shallow breathing can be a sign of anxiety or stress, while slow, deep breathing can indicate relaxation and peace. By focusing on our breathing, we anchor ourselves in the present moment, creating space for the body's signals to become more apparent.

Another important aspect of listening to the soul through the body is learning to recognize and honor our emotions. Emotions are not only mental experiences, they also manifest physically in our bodies. When we are sad, we may feel a lump in our throat or an empty feeling in our stomach. When we are angry, it is common to feel heat in our chest or tension in our muscles. Every emotion has a physical correspondence in our body, and paying attention to these sensations helps us understand what we are feeling on a deeper level. It is not about suppressing or ignoring these emotions, but rather allowing ourselves to feel them fully so we can process and release them.

The body is also a reflection of our emotional and spiritual health. Many times when we experience physical ailments or illnesses, there is an underlying emotional or spiritual cause. For example, prolonged stress can manifest itself in headaches, digestive problems, or muscle tension. Unprocessed sadness can lead to fatigue or physical weakness. Listening to our body means being attentive to these signals and asking ourselves what we really need at that moment. Sometimes, it may be rest, other times it may be talking to someone or spending time in a spiritual practice that reconnects us with ourselves.

The relationship between the soul and the body is not one-way. Just as the body reflects the state of our soul, we can also work through the body to heal the soul. Practices such as yoga, tai chi or conscious dance help us to move stagnant energy in the body and release accumulated emotional tensions. By moving the body consciously, we are also moving the energy of our soul, allowing it to flow more freely and harmoniously. These practices not only strengthen the physical body, but also give us greater mental and emotional clarity, helping us to feel more at peace and connected to ourselves.

It is important to remember that every body is unique and therefore every soul also uniquely expresses itself through the body. What may work for one person in terms of reconnecting with their body and soul may not be the same for another. The essential thing is that each of us finds the practices and tools that resonate with our inner being. It may be meditation, conscious breathing, physical exercise, or even something as simple as walking in nature. The important thing is to find a way to come back to our body, to listen to it, and to allow it to guide us to what we need for our well-being.

Another critical aspect of listening to the soul through the body is learning to respect the body's limits. Often, we push ourselves too hard, both physically and mentally, without giving the body the rest and care it needs. Ignoring these limits can lead to burnout, chronic stress, or even more serious illness. Listening to the body means being aware of when we need to rest, when we need to say no, and when it's time to let go of expectations that others, or we ourselves, have placed on our shoulders. The body has a way of letting us know when we've reached our limit, and it's our responsibility to honor those signals.

Food also plays a crucial role in the connection between soul and body. What we eat not only affects our physical health, but also our emotional and spiritual well-being. By being more aware of what we put into our bodies, we can notice how certain foods make us feel more energized and at peace, while others can make us feel heavy or irritable. By cultivating a conscious relationship with food, we listen to what our body truly needs, not only to nourish itself, but to align with our spiritual energy.

Listening to the soul through the body also involves being attentive to moments of intuition. Intuition is the voice of the soul, and it often manifests through the body as a hunch or a feeling in the stomach. It can be that sensation that tells you something isn't right, even though you can't explain it rationally. Or it can be that feeling of calm and security that guides you toward an important decision. Paying attention to these moments of intuition allows us to act in harmony with our soul and make decisions that are aligned with our true purpose.

In short, the body and soul are deeply connected, and learning to listen to the soul through the body is a skill that can transform our lives in profound and meaningful ways. Through mindfulness, respect for our emotions and boundaries, and the conscious practice of caring for our body, we can reconnect with our deepest essence and live more authentically. The body is our temple, and by listening to its signals, we are hearing the whispers of our soul, always guiding us toward what we need for our physical, emotional, and spiritual well-being.

The Power of Positive Affirmations and Conscious Thinking

Positive affirmations are a powerful tool to transform the way we think and live. At first glance, they may seem like simple phrases we repeat to ourselves, but their impact goes far beyond that. Affirmations have the ability to reprogram our mind, change our thought patterns, and as a result, influence our daily reality. When we use positive affirmations, we are training our mind to focus on what we desire, rather than what we fear or worry about.

The power behind positive affirmations lies in their ability to change our perception and focus. Our minds are like sponges; they absorb and are shaped by what we constantly repeat to them. If throughout the day we tell ourselves negative things like "I'm not enough," "I'll never make it," or "I don't deserve this," those words become our reality. However, if we consciously choose positive affirmations like "I'm capable," "I deserve the best," or "I'm on the right path," we're rewiring our minds to align with those beliefs. What we think directly affects how we feel and ultimately how we act in the world.

It's important to understand that affirmations are not just empty wishes. In order for them to work, they must be believed and deeply felt. Repeating an affirmation without conviction is like saying something for the sake of saying it, without really connecting with its meaning. In order for positive affirmations to have the desired impact, it's crucial that, when saying them, we also cultivate an internal sense of truth around them. This means that when you repeat something to yourself like "I am worthy of love and respect," you're not just saying the words, you're working to really feel and believe that this is the case.

Mindful thinking goes hand in hand with positive affirmations. This type of thinking involves being aware of what we are thinking at all times, rather than letting our mind run on autopilot. Often, we are not aware of how many negative or limiting thoughts we have throughout the day. These thoughts are often so automatic that they go unnoticed, but they affect the way we see the world and our decisions. By practicing mindful thinking, we are aware of what we are thinking, and we can quickly identify any negative or limiting patterns.

Mindful thinking is, at its core, a practice of mindfulness. It invites us to be present, to be observers of our thoughts without judgment, and to consciously choose how we want to direct our mind. When we notice that we are caught in thoughts of doubt, fear, or insecurity, we can stop, acknowledge those thoughts, and replace them with positive affirmations. It is an ongoing process of self-observation and mental readjustment that, over time, allows us to live with greater clarity, confidence, and purpose.

A simple example of how positive affirmations and conscious thinking work is when we are faced with a challenge or difficult situation. In those moments, our minds tend to fill with thoughts like "I can't handle it" or "this is too much for me." These thoughts create fear and anxiety, which often paralyzes us or leads us to avoid the challenge altogether. However, if we consciously choose in those moments to tell ourselves "I am strong," "I can handle this," or "everything is going to be okay," we change our energy and our attitude toward the situation. Suddenly, instead of feeling helpless, we begin to feel like we have control over how we react and over what is to come.

Another key aspect of the power of positive affirmations is that they help us change our perspective on ourselves and our lives. Many people carry limiting beliefs that were formed in childhood or at some point in their life, which make them believe that they are not good enough, that they do not deserve success, or that they cannot achieve what they want. These limiting beliefs act as invisible barriers that prevent us from reaching our potential. Positive affirmations work to dismantle those barriers. By repeating and reinforcing affirmations that empower us, we begin to replace those old limiting beliefs with new beliefs that support us and allow us to move forward confidently in life.

Affirmations are also a way to cultivate a mindset of gratitude and abundance. Often, when we focus on what we don't have or what we lack, we fall into a scarcity mindset, which leads to dissatisfaction and frustration. By using affirmations that reinforce gratitude, such as "I am grateful for all that I have" or "abundance flows to me naturally," we are retraining our mind to see and recognize the blessings in our lives. Not only does this make us feel happier and more at peace, but it also opens us up to receiving more of what we desire since we are aligned with positive, receptive energy.

It is essential to mention that using positive affirmations does not mean ignoring or denying the real challenges in life. It is not about pretending that everything is perfect when it is not, but rather about consciously choosing how we want to face those challenges. Affirmations allow us to adopt a proactive and positive attitude, rather than a reactive or negative one. Instead of saying "I can't" when we face an obstacle, we say "I will find a way," which empowers us and puts us on the path to solutions, rather than staying stuck in the problem.

Plus, positive affirmations have a cumulative effect. The more you practice them, the more they begin to shape your reality. At first, it may feel like a bit of a strange or forced exercise, especially if you're not used to speaking positively to yourself. But over time, you start to notice small changes. Your mindset becomes more optimistic, you feel more confident, and you start to attract more opportunities and experiences aligned with the affirmations you've been telling yourself. It's like planting a seed in your mind, which over time grows and bears fruit in the form of positive thoughts and experiences.

The key to making positive affirmations and conscious thinking work is consistency. It's not enough to repeat an affirmation once or twice and expect immediate change. It's a habit that requires daily practice. You can start your day with affirmations that inspire you, repeating them out loud or silently as you prepare for your activities. You can also use them in times of challenge, when you need a reminder of your inner strength. The important thing is to keep up the practice, even on days when you don't feel an immediate change. Over time, you'll notice that these affirmations become a part of you, shaping not only your mindset, but also the way you experience the world.

In short, the power of positive affirmations lies in their ability to transform our way of thinking and, therefore, our reality. Together with conscious thought, they give us the tools to take control of our mind, reprogram limiting beliefs, and align ourselves with a fuller, more satisfying life. By incorporating these practices into our daily lives, we not only feel more empowered, but we also create a more positive reality, in which our words and thoughts guide us towards the well-being and success we truly deserve.

Living in the Present

Living in the present is one of the most powerful keys to experiencing life in a full and meaningful way. However, while it seems simple, in practice it can be quite challenging. We often find ourselves caught up in thoughts about the past or worries about the future, which prevents us from enjoying the present moment, which is the only one we really have. We get distracted by what was or what could be, and in the process we miss the opportunity to fully live what is happening right now, in this very moment.

Life happens in the present. We cannot change what happened in the past, nor can we predict with certainty what will happen in the future. The only thing we have control over is how we choose to experience this moment. When we truly understand this, we realize that living in the present is not only important, but essential to our peace of mind and happiness. The present is where the magic of life happens. It is where our opportunities to be, to grow, to learn, and to enjoy are found.

A fundamental aspect of living in the present is mindfulness, or what is commonly called "mindfulness." This concept involves being fully attentive and engaged with what is happening in the here and now. When we are aware of the present, we immerse ourselves in our experiences without judging or labeling them, we simply live them as they are. For example, instead of quickly eating lunch while thinking about our to-do list, we can enjoy each bite, savor it, feel the texture of the food, and be grateful for the moment. This turns a simple meal into a meaningful experience.

One of the greatest enemies of living in the present is a scattered mind. Our mind is incredibly active, and if we don't train it, it tends to wander from one place to another. Sometimes we're physically in one place, but mentally we're somewhere else. We're in a conversation, but instead of listening attentively, we're thinking about what we're going to say next, or what we have to do later. This habit robs us of the ability to fully experience the present and truly connect with others and with what we're doing. The key to overcoming this habit is the conscious practice of mindfulness.

A simple exercise to begin living in the present is to focus on your breathing. Breathing is a powerful anchor that keeps you connected to the now. When you find yourself worrying about something that happened or worried about what might happen, take a few moments to breathe deeply. Inhale slowly and deeply through your nose, feeling the air filling your lungs, and then exhale slowly through your mouth. Do this several times, concentrating only on the rhythm of your breathing. You will notice that as you do this, your mind begins to calm down and your focus returns to the present. Breathing reminds us that we are here, now, and helps us move away from mental clutter.

Another important aspect of living in the present is learning to let go of control over the future. Often, our worries are born out of a desire to have everything under control. We worry about what might happen, about the outcomes we want, about things that haven't happened yet. But in reality, the future is uncertain and we can't control what will happen. We can only influence what we're doing now. When we understand this, we free ourselves from a great deal of anxiety. Instead of obsessing over what might happen, we can focus on what is in our control right now, and trust that things will unfold as they should.

Living in the present also means accepting life as it is, without fighting against what we cannot change. We often resist situations or emotions that we don't like, as if by resisting we could make them go away. But resistance only creates more stress and suffering. For example, if we are facing a difficult situation, such as a conflict at work or a personal loss, it is natural to want things to be different. However, instead of resisting or wishing for things to change immediately, we can accept the present moment as it is. This doesn't mean that we like it or resign ourselves to it, but that we stop fighting internally and accept that, in this instant, things are as they are. This acceptance frees us and allows us to act with greater clarity and wisdom.

The practice of living in the present also involves being more grateful. We often take the little things in life for granted because we are too busy thinking about what we don't have or what we lack. But when we stop to observe the present, we can discover countless reasons to feel gratitude. From the sun that shines, to the air we breathe, to the moments we share with our loved ones, it's all there, available to us if we choose to see it. Gratitude connects us deeply to the present, helping us appreciate what we have instead of mourning what isn't there.

Additionally, living in the present allows us to experience a greater sense of peace and well-being. When we let go of worries about the past and future, we free ourselves from a great deal of stress. Instead of feeling trapped in the chaos of the mind, we can find calm and serenity in the simple act of being here, now. This state of full presence is the foundation for a more balanced and conscious life. As we practice living in the present, we notice that we become more patient, more compassionate, and more connected to those around us.

It is important to understand that living in the present does not mean that we should ignore the future or stop planning. Planning is a necessary part of life, but the difference is in not letting the future become a source of constant worry. We can make plans with intention and purpose, but then we must let go of attachment to the outcomes and trust that everything will unfold according to the natural flow of life. The present is where we can truly make a difference; it is where we have the power to act, to create, to love, to learn.

Ultimately, living in the present is an art that can be cultivated with practice and patience. It's not something that can be achieved overnight, but over time, you can train your mind to be more present in each moment. Not only will this allow you to enjoy life more, but it will also give you a greater sense of inner peace and clarity. By living in the present, you align yourself with the natural flow of life, and find beauty and fulfillment in each moment, no matter what is happening around you.

Spiritual Rituals for the Mind and Soul

Spiritual rituals are practices that help us reconnect with our inner selves and with the energy around us. They are moments dedicated to nourishing both the mind and the soul, and can have a profound effect on our daily lives, helping us find peace, balance, and purpose. Although sometimes the word "ritual" can sound like something complicated or reserved only for religious practices, in reality, spiritual rituals can be as simple or complex as one wishes. The important thing is that they have meaning for us and offer us a space to reflect, feel, and be aware.

A spiritual ritual can be something as simple as lighting a candle in the morning while taking a few minutes to be thankful for the new day, or it can be a more structured practice like meditation or yoga. The key is that it is an intentional act, a moment when we disconnect from the outside noise and focus on ourselves. These rituals invite us to pause, breathe deeply, and reconnect with the essence of who we are.

One of the most common and effective rituals for the mind and soul is meditation. Meditation does not require any special skills, and anyone can begin practicing it. It simply involves sitting in silence, focusing on breathing or a positive thought, allowing the mind to calm down and the body to relax. The daily practice of meditation can have transformative effects, helping us reduce stress, increase mental clarity, and open up space within ourselves for introspection and personal growth. Over time, meditation can help us train our mind to be more present and aware of our emotions, thoughts, and experiences.

Another powerful ritual is journaling. Taking a few minutes each day to write down what you're feeling, your thoughts, your dreams, or even your worries, can be a profound way to connect with your soul. By putting your feelings into words, you clarify them and make them more manageable. Plus, writing gives you the opportunity to observe patterns in your emotions and thoughts, and this can lead to greater self-knowledge. You can also use your journal to write down your gratitude, which is a great practice for cultivating a positive attitude and staying focused on the blessings you already have in your life.

Nature can also be a powerful ally in our spiritual rituals. Spending time outdoors, whether walking through a park, sitting by a river, or simply gazing at the sky, can be a wonderful way to reconnect with the earth and find a sense of peace. This type of ritual allows us to remember that we are part of something much larger than ourselves, that we are part of the natural cycle of life. You can create a personal ritual that involves nature, such as walking barefoot in the grass in the morning, taking a few minutes to watch the sunset, or even caring for a plant at home. These simple actions can have a calming and revitalizing effect on your spirit.

Using affirmations can also be a daily spiritual practice. Affirmations are positive statements that we repeat to help us change negative thought patterns or to attract what we desire in life. You can create your own affirmations based on what you want to manifest or what you feel you need at that moment. For example, if you are seeking more inner peace, you might repeat an affirmation like, "I am at peace with myself and the world." If you want to cultivate more self-love, you might use an affirmation like, "I love and accept myself as I am." Repeating these affirmations throughout the day, or making them a morning or nighttime ritual, can help you transform your mindset and attract more positive energy into your life.

Another ritual that can be deeply spiritual is the act of letting go. Throughout our lives, we accumulate emotional burdens, resentments, and pains that, if not released, can affect our inner peace and ability to move forward. Creating a ritual to let go of these burdens can be liberating. This can be done in many ways. One option is to write down what you want to let go of on a piece of paper and then burn it, allowing the fire to symbolize the release of what you no longer need in your life. You can also do a guided visualization in which you imagine letting go of everything that weighs you down, watching it dissolve or move away from you, freeing up space for new experiences and emotions.

Sound can also be a powerful tool in spiritual rituals. Music, chanting, or even the simple act of ringing a soft bell can raise our energy vibration and help us enter a more conscious state. Tibetan singing bowls, for example, are used to harmonize the body and mind through their sound vibrations. Listening to music that inspires you or chanting mantras can also be a way to uplift your mood and open your heart. You can incorporate sound into your daily rituals, whether it's starting your day with an inspiring song or ending your day with a relaxing melody that helps you unwind from the hustle and bustle of the day.

The act of giving can also be a very meaningful spiritual ritual. When we give from the heart, whether it be our time, energy, or resources, we connect with others and with something larger than ourselves. You can create a generosity ritual where, each week, you commit to giving something without expecting anything in return. This doesn't have to be something big. It can be a gesture as simple as offering a smile, helping someone with a task, or donating to a cause you care about. By giving, we are remembering that life is a constant exchange of energy, and that by sharing what we have, we also receive in abundance.

Finally, a powerful spiritual ritual is the practice of gratitude. Being thankful for what we have and the people around us helps us cultivate a positive mindset and reminds us how lucky we are. You can make gratitude a daily ritual by taking a few minutes at the end of each day to reflect on the things you are grateful for. It doesn't matter how small the details are; the important thing is to recognize and appreciate the blessings that are present in your life. This simple act can completely change your perspective and fill you with deep inner peace.

In short, spiritual rituals for the mind and soul don't have to be complicated or grandiose. They are personal and meaningful moments that we create with the intention of reconnecting with our inner selves and the universe around us. By integrating these practices into our daily lives, we find greater clarity, peace, and purpose, and we move ever closer to a more authentic and fulfilled version of ourselves.

The Connection with Nature

Nature has an immense power to reconnect us with ourselves. In the midst of modern life, with all its distractions, it is easy to forget that we are part of this natural world, that our roots are not in concrete or screens, but in the earth, trees, air and water that surround us. Connecting with nature not only reminds us of our essence, but can also be a source of peace, healing and clarity. It is a constant reminder that we are part of a larger cycle and that everything in life is interconnected.

Simply spending time in nature, whether it's walking through a forest, sitting in a park, or just stargazing, helps us break out of our routine and find a space of calm within ourselves. Nature has a rhythm of its own, one that isn't rushed or preoccupied. By being surrounded by it, we slowly begin to tune into that slower, more peaceful rhythm. You don't need to go on long trips or adventures; sometimes a simple walk on the beach or a short hike outdoors is enough to clear your mind and feel a deep connection to the natural world.

When we spend time in nature, we may notice that our senses are awakened in a different way. The sound of the wind through the leaves, the scent of freshly cut grass, the feel of the earth beneath our bare feet—all of these connect us to the present in a very powerful way. This type of experience brings us into a state of mindfulness, where our thoughts quiet down and we begin to experience the present moment as it is, without judgment or distraction. This simple act of being in nature is a form of meditation, one that allows us to listen more deeply to our inner selves.

Connection with nature is not only physical, it is also spiritual. When we look at a landscape, whether it is majestic mountains, a meandering river, or a sky full of stars, we feel small before the immensity of creation. But that smallness is not a negative thing; on the contrary, it is a feeling that reminds us that we are part of something much bigger. We realize that nature follows its course regardless of everyday worries, and in that realization, we find peace. Seasons change, trees lose their leaves and then regain them, rivers flow constantly to the sea, and all of this happens effortlessly. Nature teaches us that there is a natural flow to life, and that by connecting with it, we can let go of control and trust the process.

Furthermore, nature is a mirror of our emotions and internal states. When we look at the calm of a lake or the fury of a storm, we can see our own feelings reflected back to us. Through this connection, nature invites us to acknowledge our emotions, to accept them and to let them flow as they are. There is no resistance in nature; everything simply is. Likewise, by connecting with nature, we can learn to accept our human experience with all its ups and downs, with all its joys and challenges, knowing that it is all part of the cycle of life.

An important aspect of this connection with nature is respect. Nature gives us so much, from the air we breathe to the food we eat, but we often take it for granted. When reconnecting with the natural world, it is also essential to cultivate a sense of gratitude and responsibility. We can do this by caring for the environment, being aware of how our actions impact the planet, and making choices that promote sustainability. This respect and gratitude not only benefits the environment, but it also benefits us, as it helps us live in harmony with the world around us.

In nature we also find important lessons about patience and resilience. A tree does not grow overnight; it takes years, even decades, to reach its size and strength. Flowers do not bloom all year round; they have their own time to open and their own time to wither. Everything in nature follows its course, slowly but surely. This is a great lesson for us, as we often want immediate results in our lives. By observing the rhythm of nature, we learn that good things take time and that each phase of life has its purpose. We learn to be patient with ourselves and our circumstances, knowing that everything has its time.

Direct contact with nature also has positive effects on our physical and mental health.

Numerous studies have shown that spending time outdoors reduces stress levels, improves mood and increases creativity. Nature has the ability to restore us, to make us feel more alive and energized. Even in the most difficult times, a walk in the woods or simply being in contact with the earth can have a healing effect. This restorative power of nature is something we have largely forgotten in our modern society, but it is available to all of us if we take the time to reconnect with it.

Finally, connecting with nature invites us to live more simply and consciously. It reminds us that we don't need so much to be happy. A sunset, birdsong, or the sound of waves crashing on the shore can bring us immense joy. By simplifying our lives and being more present in the moment, we can find a deeper satisfaction that comes from being in tune with the natural world and with ourselves.

In short, connecting with nature is a gateway to a fuller, more conscious and balanced life. It offers us the opportunity to reconnect with our essence, to learn from the cycles of life and to find peace in simplicity. By taking the time to be in contact with the natural world, we not only benefit ourselves, but we also contribute to the preservation of that world, creating a relationship of respect and gratitude with the earth that sustains us.

Finding and Living Your Life Mission

Finding your life mission is one of the most important journeys we can undertake. It is not about something external or meeting other people's expectations, but about discovering what truly resonates within you, what fills you with purpose and motivates you every day to get up and move forward. Many times, people wonder what their purpose in the world is, and although it may seem like something difficult to find, the truth is that your life mission is already within you, waiting to be discovered. It is a process of self-knowledge, listening to your heart and aligning yourself with what you are most passionate about and what makes you feel fulfilled.

The first step to finding your life mission is to pause and reflect. In our day-to-day lives, it's easy to get distracted by responsibilities, social expectations, and everyday tasks, but to connect with your mission, it's essential to create a space of calm and silence where you can listen to yourself. This reflection isn't always immediate. Sometimes it can take time, but simply taking a few minutes a day to think about what really matters to you and how you want to contribute to the world can be very revealing.

It's helpful to start with basic questions: What do I enjoy doing most? What activities make me lose track of time? What issues or causes am I deeply passionate about? How would I like to be remembered? These questions invite you to dig into what drives you, what truly sparks a spark within you. Maybe you enjoy helping others, or maybe you feel a deep connection to art, nature, teaching, or innovation. No matter what your answer is, the important thing is that it comes from deep within you, from your authentic desires and not from what you think you "should" do.

Once you begin to identify those things you are passionate about, the next step is to look for ways to integrate those passions into your daily life. Many people make the mistake of thinking that their life mission has to be directly related to their job or profession, but that is not always the case. While it would be ideal for your calling and your mission to be aligned, you can also live out your purpose in many other ways. You can do this through personal projects, volunteering, hobbies, or simply being a source of support and love for the people around you. The most important thing is that you find ways to express your mission, no matter the context.

Living your life mission doesn't mean that everything will always be easy. There will be obstacles and moments when you doubt yourself, but it is in those moments that it is most important to remember why you started. Having a clear purpose will give you the strength and motivation to overcome difficulties, because you will know that what you do has a greater meaning. It is not just a matter of external success or recognition, but of feeling aligned with your inner truth.

A key aspect of finding your mission is patience. Sometimes the answers don't come right away, and that's okay. You don't have to have it all figured out in one day. The important thing is to keep exploring, to keep looking for signs and clues to guide you. Often, the signs of our life's mission come at unexpected times: a conversation with a friend, a book that comes into your hands at just the right moment, an experience that changes your perspective. Stay open to these signs and trust that, little by little, the path will become clearer.

In addition to listening to your heart, it's also important to pay attention to your talents and abilities. We all have unique gifts that we can share with the world. Some people are great communicators, others have a natural ability to solve problems or create beautiful things. Identifying your gifts is key to discovering how you can put them to use for others. Remember that your mission is not just something that benefits you, but something that can also have a positive impact on the world. Living your mission is about contributing to the lives of others in a way that only you can, with your talents, your perspective, and your unique energy.

Sometimes our life mission can also be related to overcoming challenges or hardships. You may have gone through difficult experiences that taught you valuable lessons, and those lessons can be the key to helping others who are going through similar situations. Many times, our purpose is found in our own stories of healing and transformation. What you have experienced and what you have learned along the way can be a gift to others.

Living your life mission also involves making conscious choices. Once you discover what you truly want and what gives you meaning, it's important to act on it. This may require changes in your lifestyle, your job, or your relationships. Sometimes, it can be scary to step out of your comfort zone, but living in alignment with your purpose is worth it. Every step you take toward your mission, no matter how small, is a step toward a more authentic and fulfilling life.

It's also important to remember that your life mission isn't static. Over time, your interests, passions, and skills can evolve, and with them, so can your mission. Don't worry if what you're passionate about today changes in the future. The key is to remain true to yourself and be willing to adapt to new paths that open up before you. Living your mission is an ongoing process of self-discovery and growth.

Finally, an essential part of living your mission is gratitude. Being grateful for every step of the way, both the achievements and the challenges, will help you maintain a positive and open attitude. Gratitude reminds you that every experience, good or bad, is part of your journey and is bringing you closer to your purpose. Be grateful for the opportunities that present themselves, the people who support you, and the lessons you learn. When you live with gratitude, you align yourself with an energy of abundance that attracts more opportunities and blessings into your life.

In short, finding and living your life mission is a process of self-knowledge, patience, and action. It doesn't happen overnight, but each step you take brings you closer to a full and meaningful life. Listen to your heart, follow your passions, use your gifts, and stay open to the signs of the universe. Your mission is already within you, waiting to be discovered.

When you find it, you will feel a deep satisfaction and a sense of purpose that will guide you through every step of your life.